SUPPORT

POWER!

BUY THIS BOOK...

AND CONTRIBUTE TO THE FIGHT AGAINST:

Bull-Throwing Advertisers

Sexploiting Movie-Makers

Condescending TV Networks

Irresponsible Publishers

Self-Serving Politicians

Polluting Industry

Destructive Militants

Pseudo-Patriots

Inept Labor

Indifferent Parents

...AND MOST IMPORTANT OF ALL...

Poverty

(MAINLY OURS!)

MAD POWER

Edited by
Albert B. Feldstein

WARNER BOOKS

A Time Warner Company

WARNER BOOKS EDITION

Copyright © 1964 and 1977 by E.C. Publications, Inc.

All rights reserved.
No part of this book may be reproduced without permission.
For information address:
E.C. Publications, Inc.
485 Madison Ave.
New York, N.Y. 10020.

**Title "MAD" used with permission of its owner,
E.C. Publications, Inc.**

This Warner Books Edition is published by
arrangement with E.C. Publications, Inc.

**Warner Books, Inc.
666 Fifth Avenue
New York, N.Y. 10103**

W A Time Warner Company

Printed in the United States of America

First Printing: December, 1977

Reissued: December, 1991

10 9 8 7 6

MAD POWER

A while back, "The IN and OUT Book" by Harvey Schmidt and Robert Benton showed us what was currently "IN" and what was "OUT". To be IN, a thing has to be either classic and great, like Barbra Streisand — or very obscure, like Lyle Bettger movies—or so far out that even the OUT people (Squares) wouldn't touch it, like Guy Lombardo records. But these were based upon the opinions of two sophisticated adults with excellent taste. We at MAD have our own standards of judgment. We therefore feel it our duty to present our own versions of what's IN and what's OUT. So here we go with

The MAD IN and OUT Book

Written by Arnie Kogen
Illustrated by Paul Coker, Jr.

Autumn in New York and Paris in the Spring are OUT.

Winter in Hoboken is IN, but not if you live there

Being a high school drop out is OUT... unless you're a high school teacher.

Surfing is OUT.

Asking the kids over to throw the javelin is IN.

Beards and goatees are OUT.

Handlebar mustaches are IN, but not for men.

The Twist, the Hully-Gully, the Monkey, the Surf, the Ska and the Frug are all OUT.

Doing the Limbo under barbed wire is IN.

Calling your girl from home is OUT.

Speaking to her in a phone booth is IN. (If a crowd gathers, however, the both of you should step out and let somebody else use the booth!)

aving an upset stomach,
virus or a cold is OUT.

Suffering from the Plague
or Potato Famine is IN.
(It is very IN to call in
sick with Potato Famine!)

"Time," "Life," "Look"
and "Playboy" are OUT!

"Field and Stream" is IN
... but only for pin-ups!

Getting the Hiccoughs
while making out is IN.

Swallowing goldfish
and piling into
phonebooths is OUT.

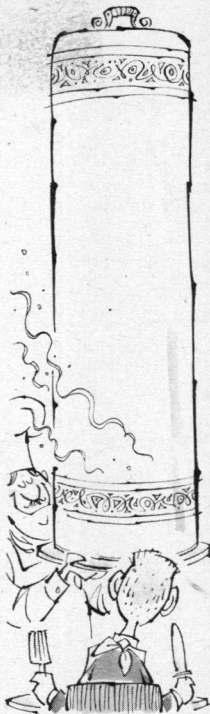

Newest IN campus
craze is swallowing
phonebooths.

When he calls, having
your folks say you're
in is OUT. Having them
say you're out is IN —
but only if you're in.

Becoming an engineer, an accountant, a lawyer, or a doctor is OUT.

The new IN careers are: Gas Lamp Lighter, Ice Man, Shepherd, and Seltzer Truck Driver.

Singing along with Mitch is OUT.

Singing along with The Eleven O'Clock News is IN ... but only if you hum along with The Weather.

Going to a Drive-In Movie with your date is OUT.

It's only IN when you take her there in a Taxi Cab!

Walking barefoot in the rain is OUT.

Wearing golashes in the house is IN.

Water sports in ocean, lake or pool are OUT.

Water Skiing through a swamp is IN. Also Scuba Diving in quicksand.

Shaving with Stainless Steel blades is IN.

Shaving with "Coo-Coo" Razor blades is OUT.

When playing Monopoly, owning "Boardwalk" and "Park Place" is OUT.

Staying in "Jail" for the entire game is IN.

Calling a girl Monday for a Saturday date is OUT.

Also, calling Saturday afternoon for Saturday night is no longer as IN as it used to be.

Sorry, I'm busy.

2000 APRIL

Newest IN dating technique: Calling Sunday for Saturday, the day before. (Hi, Baby, are you busy yesterday?)

Also very IN—calling to make a date way in advance. (Could I see you, say, at the turn of the century?)

Submitting quietly to an
Army Induction Physical is OUT.

Being carried away screaming is
IN. Especially if you're a girl.

Going to Europe is IN
... but only if you row there.

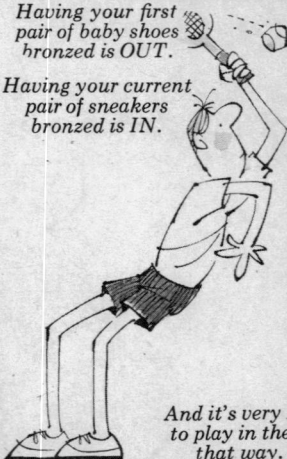

Having your first
pair of baby shoes
bronzed is OUT.

Having your current
pair of sneakers
bronzed is IN.

And it's very IN
to play in them
that way.

Edsels are so far out, they're IN.

HONEST JOHN

Driving sports cars like Ferraris, Jaguars, Maseratis and Dual Ghias are OUT.

*When the lights are low
and she expects mood music,
playing "The Caisson Song" is IN.*

Kaiser Frazers are IN. Also picking up your date in a 1958 Hearse is very IN.

Going to a Motel is OUT.

Going to an Inn is IN.

Hamburgers, pizzas and hot dogs are OUT.

Cod liver oil, tripe and Farina are IN.

Also very IN—
drinking hot tea through a straw.

And the most IN of all are Bread Sandwiches, like rye on roll with a side of whole wheat.

Have you noticed the interesting money-making schemes that grace the pages of our magazines nowadays? A group of famous people in a particular field get together and form a correspondence school to teach hopefuls who want to enter that field some of the tricks of the trade. First came the "Famous Artists School"—then came "The Famous Writers School"—followed by "The Famous Cartoonists School"—and now "The Famous Photographers School." If this trend keeps up, we should be seeing some rather unusual

Famous People's Home-Study Courses

ARTIST: BOB CLARKE
WRITER: AL JAFFEE

FIRST "FAMOUS PEOPLE'S HOME-STUDY COURSE"

America's 12 Most Famous Artists

ALBERT DORNE

NORMAN ROCKWELL

JON WHITCOMB

AL PARKER

HAROLD VON SCHMIDT

STEVAN DOHANOS

FRED LUDEKENS

PETER HELCK

ROBERT FAWCETT

BEN STAHL

GEORGE GIUSTI

AUSTIN BRIGGS

"We're looking for people who like to draw"

By ALBERT DORNE
Famous Magazine Illustrator

Do you like to draw or paint? If you do—America's 12 Most Famous Artists are looking for you. We'd like to help you find out if you have talent worth developing.

Here's why we make this offer. More than a decade ago, my colleagues and I realized that too many people were missing wonderful careers in art . . . either because they hesitated to think they had talent . . . or because they couldn't get top-notch professional art training without leaving home or giving up their jobs.

A Plan to Help Others

We decided to do something about this. First, we pooled the rich, practical experience, the professional know-how, and the precious trade secrets that helped us reach the top. Then—illustrating this knowledge with over 5,000 special drawings and paintings—we created a complete course of art training that folks all over the country could take right in their own homes and in their spare time. This course is accredited by the Accrediting Commission, National Home Study Council, Washington, D. C., a nationally recognized accrediting agency.

Our training has helped thousands of men and women win the creative satisfactions and the cash rewards of part-time or full-time art careers. Here are just a few:

Herb Smith was a payroll clerk. Soon after he started studying with us, he landed an art job with a large printing firm. This was four years ago; today he's head artist for the same firm.

Helps Design New Cars

Halfway through our training, Don Golemba of Detroit landed a job in the styling department of a major automobile company. Now he helps design new car models.

"Your course has been the difference between failure and success for me," writes Robert Meechan of Ontario, Canada. "I've come from an $18.00 a week apprentice to where I now own my own home, two cars, and hold stock in two companies."

John Whitaker of Memphis was an airline clerk when he began studying with us. Recently, a huge syndicate signed him to do a daily comic strip.

Earns Seven Times as Much

Eric Ericson of Minneapolis was a clerk when he enrolled with us. Now, he heads an advertising-art-studio business and earns *seven times* his former salary.

Elizabeth Lincoln—mother of six —now teaches art classes in her Massachusetts home. She's building a tidy nest egg for the education of her children.

Cowboy Starts Art Business

Donald Kern—a Montana cowboy —studied with us. Now he paints portraits, sells them for $250 each. And he gets all the business he can handle.

Gertrude Vander Poel had never drawn a thing until she started studying with us. Now a swank New York gallery exhibits her paintings for sale.

Free Art Talent Test

How about you? Wouldn't you like to find out if you have talent worth training for a full-time or part-time art career? Simply send for our revealing 12-page talent test. Thousands paid $1 for this test, but we'll send it to you *free*. If you show promise, you'll be eligible for at-home training under the program we direct. No obligation. Mail the coupon today.

When the field of illustration was killed by photography, a group of desperate illustrators introduced a home-study course with advertisements that stressed the money-making opportunities for artists. This proved to be true—as the swelling bank accounts of the school's founders will show.

LATEST "FAMOUS PEOPLE'S HOME-STUDY COURSE"

When photography replaced illustration, anyone who could snap a shutter got into the act. The field is now crowded and competition is fierce. Seeing the handwriting on the wall, several apprehensive photographers are now trying the same trick that saved some of their former victims.

Bitsko Osszefogva Cowznofski Finster Sturdley

Freem Furd Carbuncle Bluebeard Neuman

Ten famous butchers start home-study course

Now—the most exciting, secure vocation this country can offer

If you are too young to remember World War II, a little research will quickly reveal that the most powerful, most sought-after person on the home front was the family butcher. No one ate better or made more money in what has come to be remembered nostalgically as "The Black Market". In fact, so much meat was sold under the counter in those days that three out of four butchers developed permanent curvature of the spine from bending down so much.

Now, with war a constant threat, the butcher's big day could return at any moment. You wouldn't want to miss out on all that, would you? And even if there is no war, you won't find a healthier, more secure bunch than butchers. Their average weight of 238 pounds will attest to this, because every pound comes from eating prime cuts—the kind their customers never get to see.

So plan on starting your own business as a butcher today. Write now for this marvelous course. It comes in 18 Easy-To-Follow Lessons, and we even supply the special leakproof bags for you to ship your homework to us in.

Famous Butchers School
Dept. 85, Hamhock, Illinois

Name ....
Address ....
City .... State ....

18

Kirby

Gabor

Jessel

Francis

Parks

Genvieve

Clark

Daly

Linkletter

Neuman

Ten famous celebrities start home-study course

Now—you can be famous without doing a single outstanding thing

Up until now, becoming famous was limited to those individuals who accomplished something of great distinction, either through years of hard work, or by the application of rare talent. But now at last, you can become famous without doing one single thing to deserve it. Proof that this can be accomplished is graphically demonstrated by the ten famous members of our faculty. Every one of them is a celebrity for no apparent reason that anyone can think of. Now if they can do it, why can't you?

Yes, let these eminently qualified experts in this field teach you how. The course they present is simplicity itself. Everything our famous founders stand for — everything they know — everything they've done to deserve their fame has been compressed into one single easy-to-learn lesson. In fact, it's been compressed into one single easy-to-learn word. Aren't you dying to learn that one word that can start you on the road to fame and fortune? Write today!

19

Rockefeller
Hartford
Hughes
Zeckendorf
Getty
Hunt
Hefner
Gaines
Neuman

Ten famous millionaires start home-study course

Now—no matter how wretched or poor a slob you are—you can learn to live like a millionaire

How often have you dreamed of being a millionaire—of enjoying the same experiences and prestige and security that millionaires enjoy? Well, now you don't need a million dollars to attain all this. Let these ten famous millionaires teach you everything they know by mail. A modest fee, in 75 monthly installments, will bring you all the intimate details. You will learn how millionaires live, eat, sleep and play through this remarkable home-study course. For example, Lesson #9 is a full length color movie depicting the pleasure domes that millionaires frequent. Watching this is like going on a vacation you never dreamed you could afford. And Lesson #17 contains full-size cardboard

color prints of the interiors of millionaire mansions. Pasted onto your shabby walls, you will feel what millionaires feel as they sit amid resplendant luxury. And Lesson #28 is a stereophonic tape of a gala millionaire party. You hear the actual voices of the people with whom millionaires socialize—people making clever, witty, wealthy talk. Doesn't that sound splendid? And just think: If you do happen to become a millionaire through some trick of fate, you'll be able to slide right into it so much more gracefully after taking this wonderful course. Enroll today.

Ferris
Carpenter
Grissom
Glenn
Shepard
Schirra
Jimenez
Laika
Neuman

Ten famous space travellers start home-study course

Now—no matter what your physical condition—you can learn to conquer space

If you want to experience the thrill of space travel and the consequent glamour of ticker tape parades in your honor, then this course is for you. Let ten famous space travelers teach you the intimate first-hand details right in your own home . . . and in only 12 easy lessons. So easy, in fact, that many of our best students are under 12 years of age. And it's pleasant, too. No tiresome months of backbreaking exercise. No endless hours of sickening testing and training. No monotonous diets of space food. Just one half hour a day does the trick with this marvelous course. After 12 weeks, you will know everything that many of our famous space travelers know . . . specifically those in pictures 3, 6 and 9, above. Then you'll be ready for space flights whenever openings show up in the near future. Write now to:

21

Feldstein

Putnam

Brenner

De Fuccio

Meglin

Tirado

Andthe

Usualgang

Ofidiots

Neuman

Ten famous swindlers start home-study course

Now—you can learn to cheat, embezzle, defraud—and then live a glorious life abroad

You have doubtlessly heard the expression "Crime does not pay!" Well, it really *doesn't* if you bother with low-class crimes like burglary, mugging, pickpocketing, etc. But just think for a moment of how often you've read about a politician, for example, whose salary is, say $15,000 a year, and after three years in office, he's worth $9,000,000. There's a big stir for a while, the politician resigns, the thing blows over, and he lives happily and wealthily ever after. That's class. And that's what our ten expert instructors have in common.

Many of them, the best shady money-making brains in the world, were heretofore unavailable to eager students. Only through this home-study course can we now offer the talents of some of the world's great citizens who are living in luxury and safety in countries that do not have extradition laws. At last, these highly-respected swindlers are ready to share their secrets with you. Enroll now and learn how you can live out your years spending other people's money in some far-off Utopia.

Batton Barton Durstine Doyle Dane

Bernbach Foote Cone Belding Neuman

Ten famous ad men start home-study course

Now—no matter how stupid or untalented you are, you can make it big in the advertising game

At last—the real low-down from these ten highly-qualified ad men. What makes them so highly qualified, you ask? Is it because of the big accounts they've handled? Is it because of the new concepts in sales and promotions they've created? Have they written memorable slogans or otherwise added to the prestige of advertising? The answer is a resounding NO! On the contrary, they were clientless failures who were about to close up shop when a group of dazed and ragged illustrators staggered into their agency several years ago with a hair-brained scheme for starting a correspondence school. As a last fling into what

should have been certain failure, they brainstormed up one of their typically simpleminded, uninspired ads with the headline, "Ten famous illustrators start home-study course". Well, the rest is history. The idea caught on, the money poured in, and they became famous for this type of advertising. But now, other ad agencies are getting into the act with other correspondence schools, and the future is beginning to look black. So they decided to offer this home-study course which teaches how to write ads for home-study courses. Enroll today!

23

SCHLOOT

FLOT

FLÁDAT

FLIT

27

Valentine's Day is a time to show feelings of love and affection. And who is more worthy of receiving our love than the folks who receive all of our money . . . namely American Industry. So, with this heartfelt sentiment to guide us, let us now demonstrate our affection with . . .

MAD's Valentines to American Industry

WRITER: FRANK JACOBS

To The Designers of Women's Fashions:

Dear Valentine!

Your dresses hang like burlap sacks;
Your coats are a disgrace;
Your hats might well have been designed
For use in outer space;
Before you make up next year's styles
To sell your faithful harem—
Please have some pity on us guys
Who have to watch girls wear 'em!

ARTIST: JACK RICKARD

To The
Makers of Electrical Appliances

Dear Valentine!

Your new electric toothbrush just
Destroyed Ma's upper plate;
Your new electric blanket just
Ignited Uncle Nate;
Your new electric mixer won't
Let go of little Sue;
Each day we're finding brand-new things
Appliances can do!

ARTIST: DON MARTIN

To The

Bell

Telephone
System:

We once adored you, Valentine,
But now you've made us sore—
With numbers like six-one-five-nine-
Four-two-eight-six-three-four;
We feel that we've been led astray,
You've treated us so sloppily;
But that's the price we have to pay
When using a monopoly!

To The
Makers Of
Headache
Remedies:

Whenever we have headache ills,
We try to end our sufferin
With aspirin and other pills
Like Anacin and Bufferin;
But, Valentine, we must endure
The pains, because you see—
We get the headaches
     watching your
Commercials on TV!

To The TV Networks!

Oh, Valentine, your shows this year
Cannot be beat for dumbness;
Because of you, our senses reel;
Our minds are filled with numbness;

And yet it's sort of nice to know
That viewers 'cross the nation
Can all enjoy your shows with just
a pre-school education!

ARTIST: MORT DRUCKER

To The Automobile Companies:

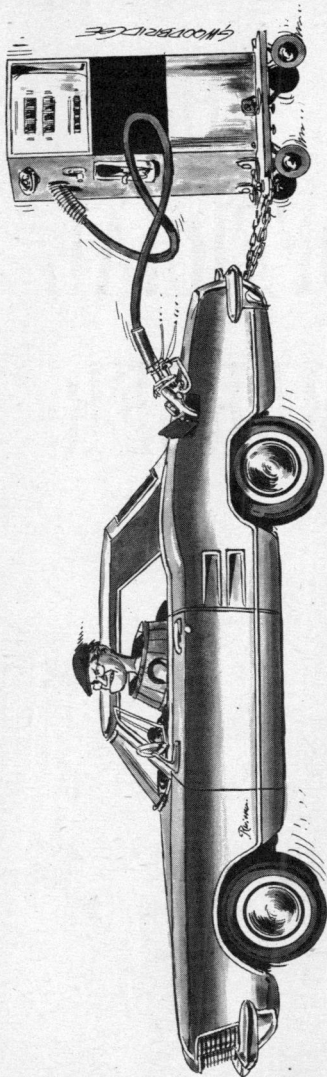

You give your cars real fancy names
Like Tempest, Riviera;

Like Comet, Skylark, Galaxie,
LeSabre and Polara;

Your names are helpful, Valentine,
Because each year we're learning—

The fancier a car is named,
The more gas it is burning!

ARTIST: GEORGE WOODBRIDGE

35

THE OFFICIAL BARBER

SKREEEE

CLIK·CLIK·CLIK·CLIK·CLIK

VOW

GRRR

38

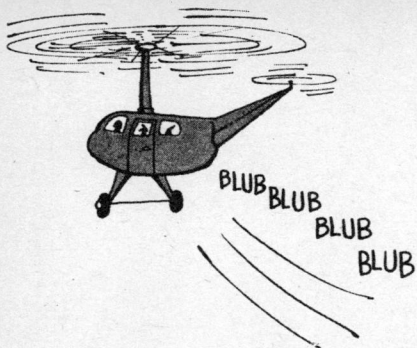

SNIP

Nowadays, when you go to the movies, you see sickness, violence, murder . . . and that's only the cartoon! Films today have deep psychological meanings and shock endings. What ever happened to all the good old movies where you knew the ending long before you entered the theater, but you sat there engrossed, anyway? Today, when Hollywood speaks of *"monster"* movies, they mean anything starring Tuesday Weld. In the good old days, when they spoke of *"monster"* movies, they meant such great flicks as "King Kong," "Son of Kong" and "Mighty Joe Young." And so, in an attempt to bring back the good old days, MAD proudly presents:

SON OF
MIGHTY JOE
KONG

STARRING:

JAMES GARNER	DORIS DAY	DICK VAN DYKE
as	as	as
Robert Headstrong	Rae Faye	Bruce Cabbage

and **RICHARD BURTON** in his greatest character role as the

SON OF
MIGHTY JOE KONG

Illustrated by Mort Drucker   Written by Dick De Bartolo

But— I'm only **human!** The strain is **too much!** Drums! Drums! **Drums!** Pulsating rhythms pounding faster than my heart . . . !

Get **hold** of yourself, Rae! You're doing that bit **much too early!** The drums have been beating for only **20 seconds!**

I have a **low** breaking point!

BOOM BOOM BOOM

The drums are coming from over here behind these tall weeds! Let's **peek!!**

Eee-gads! Savages performing pagan rituals handed down through the centuries!

Did you ever see a lassie . . . Go this way and that way? Did you ever see a lassie . . . Go this way and that . . . ??

This is dangerous territory we're in, Rae! I'm sorry we got you—**a woman**—involved! Your place is at home where it's safe and warm and . . .
I can do anything you **men** can do! So don't think of me as a **woman!** Think of me as . . . a **very sexy man!**

All right, Rae! We **believe** you can do anything we men can do! **But . . . shaving is ridiculous! !**
Which one of you guys has my **after-shave?**
Enough of this, Bob! We've got to figure a way to get **out** of this terrible place!

BONNNNNGGG

There it is again!

Twice!? That can mean only one thing . . . ! It's two o'clock!!

ROARRRR

Two o'clock, nothing! I'm taking a wild guess, but I'll bet that was the signal calling for the legendary giant ape SON OF MIGHTY JOE KONG!!

It's either that, or this movie will have to have a different title!

TARZAN SLEEPS HERE

48

Those **drums!** Those **incessant** drums—beating, **beating!!**

Enough is **enough,** already, Rae! Now you and Kong go out there and **stamp** your way into the hearts of that audience . . .

. . . while **we** pray that the **stage** doesn't **collapse!**

RAT-TAT-TAT

Just me and my shadow . . . strolling down the avenue . . . Me and my shadow . . . all alone and feeling blue . . .*

Sensational!

Great!

That ape certainly knows how to **ape!**

Best 40-foot dancing ape I ever **saw!**

* "ME AND MY SHADOW," © 1927 BY BOURNE, INC.

Those flash bulbs are driving him **crazy!** He's breaking loose!!

Quick! Get Kong's contract! I'm **sure** it doesn't have an **Escape Clause** . . .

I've heard of people walking out on **bad performances** . . . but this is **ridiculous!!**

53

That's no Hula-Hoop! It's a Wedding Band! For —sob— **KONG!!**

For **KONG!?**

Yes, I'm in **love** with him! I was going to ask him to **marry** me!

You and Kong— **married!** Rae, that's **crazy! Insane! Absurd!** You know you come from different racial and religious backgrounds!

And think of your future **Mother-In-Law!** I know they're supposed to be beasts, but yours will be ridiculous!

Telegram!

It's from Kong!! It says . . .

"Dear Rae, Bob and Bruce: New York is not for me! I'm heading for that place where I can run wild and free, unchained and unnoticed, where there are no laws and no customs to keep me tied down. Yes, I'm heading for that savage, dog-eat-dog land, Hollywood, California!"

Signed: "M. J. K."!

I NEED ALL THE FRIENDS I CAN GET

Good ol' Charlie Schulz has done it again! The creator of Peanuts has come out with his third book. This one tells how great friends are when you're a kid...i.e. "A friend is someone who will hold a place in line for you." and "A friend is someone who sticks up for you when you're not there." Well, MAD has done it again, too. Mainly, we remember childhood not so much by the friends we had, but by the finks we could do without. And so, here is our third parody of Mr. Schulz's books:

I GOT ALL THE FINKS I NEED

59

ARTIST: BOB CLARKE   WRITER: LARRY SIEGEL

A fink is that polite kid from
next door who your parents
always want to know why
you can't be as nice as.

A fink is a kid sister who
has to go every place you go.

A fink is someone
who turns in an alarm
when the school is on fire.

A fink is a
"Hide-And-Go-Seek"
base-sticker.

A fink is a mother
who vacuums during
your favorite TV show.

A fink is a neat older brother
who never ruins his clothes
so that you have to wear
everything he outgrows.

A fink is someone
who talks to a teacher
after class.

A fink is someone
who gives you the measles
during summer vacation.

A fink is a smart-aleck girl
who reminds the teacher that
she forgot to give out the
homework assignment.

A fink is someone who visits you
when you're sick in order to
play with your new toys.

A fink is a classmate
who won't let you copy
his homework.

A fink is a teammate who
goes home the first time his
mother calls him.

A fink is someone who,
when you're playing
ball and you miss one
and you yell "Get a
ball!" -- doesn't.

A fink is someone who dares to
knock something off your shoulder
after you dare him to knock
something off your shoulder.

A fink is someone who
licks all the sprinkles
off his ice cream cone
before offering you a taste.

A fink is a maid who puts your pants
in the washing machine and forgets
to take your grasshopper collection
out of the back pocket.

A fink is a kid you beat up every day who won't make friends
with you after he has a swimming pool built in his backyard.

A fink is a former friend
who becomes drunk with power
when he's made a stairway monitor.

A fink is a lefty who
uses a right-handed mitt
on the wrong hand while you
have to play barehanded.

A fink is someone
who sits next to you
and gets carsick !

A fink is a smiling doctor with a needle behind his back.

A fink is someone who runs a snowplow.

A fink is a cowboy who kisses.

A fink is a dog who chews up your Beatles Magazine instead of your father's new shoes.

SHAM-POOH DEPT.

Today is the era of the "Specialized Magazine." For the man who wishes he were the outdoor type, there's "Field & Stream"; for the guy who would love to be a swinging bachelor, there's "Playboy"; for the gal who wants to stay young and alluring, there's "Seventeen." All these magazines have one thing in common: They offer **vicarious wish-fulfillments** to their readers. In other words, they appeal to people who **wish** to be someone they're **not**. (F'instance, if you already **were** a swinging bachelor, you wouldn't **have** to read "Playboy." You wouldn't even have **time** for it!) Which brings us to the premise of this here article: Why not put out a magazine to appeal to all the people who are trying desperately to be someone they're not . . . or to put it more earthy, **the phonies?** Here then is the ultimate in "Specialized Magazines"—the one with mass appeal because it hits **everybody** . . .

To Drop At Parties

* * *

P H O N Y ' S
Checklist Of
Obscure Authors Worth
Mentioning—But Not
Worth Reading

* * *

**50 INCONSPICUOUS
THINGS TO DO TO
ATTRACT ATTENTION**

* * *

Those Ridiculously
P H O N Y
Hollywood-Type Parties
—And How To Throw One

* * *

**HOW TO TELL IF A
"TOM SWIFTY"
IS MERELY "GREAT!" OR
REALLY BEAUTIFUL!**

* * *

SPECIAL FEATURE

Full-Color Fold-Out Picture Of
"The Phony Of The Month"
Trying To Impress People
That He's Ignoring PLAYBOY's
Full-Color Fold-Out Picture Of
"The Playmate Of The Month"

* * *

EXCLUSIVE
PHONY MAGAZINE
INTERVIEWS CASSIUS CLAY
and even we can't take it!

*"How To Turn Your Disgusting Hovel
Into A Pop Art Museum"—See page 59*

GARBAGE

DIRTY
DISHES

DIRTY
WINDOW

Campbell
SOUP

UNMADE BED!!!

PHONY LABELS
Ten for $1⁰⁰

Want a reputation as the "Smartest Dressed Woman" in your group? It's simple and costs so little. Just send **$1.00** to PHONY, Box **7**, and we will supply you with 10 labels from exclusive shops like "Balmain," "Givenchy" and "St. Laurent." Sew them inside any old rag and this subtle play will make you a "Fashion Plate." Or — if you feel subtlety is wasted on your group, you can always sew the labels on the **outside** of your clothes!

IT'S NOT WHAT YOU KNOW THAT'S IMPORTANT,
IT'S HOW YOU SAY IT!

Wouldn't you like to be the center of attention at the next party? Does the fact that you dropped out of grade school make you feel inadequate? You can change all that in only six minutes a day with—

PHONY ACCENT LESSONS

Yessiree, it's not *what* you say that's important, it's *how* you say it. With a Phony British Accent, for example, what was once scorned as grossly ignorant opinions becomes words of wisdom. Remember, someone with a British Accent sounds better reading a Phone Book than an American reading the Gettysburg Address!

SEND $5.00 TO "PHONY ACCENT LESSONS," BOX 9

Phonies Around Town
by Lovely Persons

Friends of Doris Dean say she looks absolutely marvelous. Seems she recently dyed her hair silver blue, and now looks like a mature 30-year-old. Since darling Doris is only 18, that's about as "Phony" as you can get . . . Did you see the wonderfully shocked look on Sid Carom's face when he walked into his *"Surprise Party"* last Saturday night? Well, Sid was even more shocked when he suddenly realized that his best pal, Joe Kornblatt, wasn't there. Seems Sid had forgotten to invite him . . . The Rock Rodneys (He's the up-and-coming film star) have decided on a reconciliation. It appears their impending divorce didn't get enough publicity in the press.

* * * * * *

Silly Kid Dept.: Gossip columnist Earl Witless was fired last week for printing an item in his column that he *didn't* make up. If we want facts, Earl, we'll read them in the front pages . . . What's with Mae Ludwig? She was seen in church last Sunday—praying, instead of comparing hats! Just a phase, we hope, Mae... Talk about class, catch Ginny Gan doing her morning shopping at the A & P in her toreador pants, spike heels and mink stole.

* * * * * *

Headscratcher Dept.: What was Phyllis Duncan thinking of when she actually looked at her partner while dancing a Cha-Cha? . . . Rita Martin gets our vote for the "Hostess-With-The-Mostess." She had 18 people for a 12 course dinner last Thursday, and told them, "Oh, it's just something I whipped up!" Stu Betts wins admiring glances from his fellow passengers whenever he flies jet. As the plane takes off, he always pretends he's napping instead of praying . . . Talk about "chic"! For three straight weeks, Pauline Fields has had a token representative from a different minority group at her Friday night parties.

* * * * * *

Starting Young Dept.: Hats off to the gang of 12-year-olds of the Yonkers Bears Little League Team who lost 110-0 and then gave a team cheer for their opponents after the game instead of hating their guts . . . Kudos for funeral director Fred Graham, whose observation, "He died so young!" comforted the family at the funeral of 95-year-old Asa Kreevich last week . . . Phil Lorn has left his position as "Communications Specialist" (messenger boy) for a post as "Information Promulgator" (messenger boy).

* * * * * *

Best Laid Plans, Etc. Dept.: Starlet Vivian Smooch was frustrated in her attempt to sneak out of New York unnoticed. Seems her helicopter developed engine trouble and was unable to take off from Times Square during the Rush Hour . . . Debbie Fleischer has put an end to the rumor that she'll star in a Broadway play this fall. She stopped spreading it . . . Dolph Colon, the movie censor, has decided to ban "Pasta La Vita", the new Italian film import. "After seeing it 11 times, I feel that it is pornographic and offensive to decent people," Dolph told me in an exclusive interview. "But I want to see it 5 or 6 more times to make *sure!*"

* * * * * *

An inspiration to phony tots everywhere is the 6-year-old who told Macy's Department Store Santa Claus, "All I want for Christmas is World Peace and good health for my family!"... Hats off to filmland phony, Steve Ripple, who says he would gladly scrap his new $250,000 movie contract to do a worthwhile Off-Broadway Show. Atta boy, Steve . . . And now, in the sincere and immortal words of Red Skelton, after he has finished a bad taste TV sketch—"Thanks for inviting me into your living room, good-night and God bless..."

Arthur
Glusky

"Phony Of The
Month" Award

THE PHONY
OF THE MONTH

PHONY MAGAZINE follows Arthur Glusky, winner of "The Phony Of The Month" Award, through a typical day in his phony life.

Arthur starts his day off right with a phrase like, "You're beautiful! You're a beautiful guy!"—said to the mirror.

At work, he walks past the secretary, saying loud enough for all to hear, "Hold all calls, Miss Smerch!" before Miss Smerch can say, "Arthur, will you stop walking through the Boss's office to get to your job in the mailroom?"

At lunchtime, Arthur quickly gobbles the egg salad sandwiches his mother's made for him. Then he leaves the stockroom and spends the remaining 50 minutes in front of a fancy restaurant, casually picking his teeth. Naturally, people who pass think he ate in *there*.

On the way home, Arthur hides behind his paper and plays "The Rush Hour Game" or "If I don't see you, Old Lady, you're really not there!" But, 3 stops before his, Arthur lowers his paper, spots the old lady, and gives her his seat. Then, he promptly gets lost in the crowd and gets off unnoticed... a real fine boy.

That night, when Arthur calls for his
date, he immediately ingratiates him-
self with the girl's parents — telling
the girl's mother, "I can see where
Irene gets her good looks!" . . . this
after having just finished telling the
exact same thing to the girl's father.

After Arthur strikes out with his date,
he meets the boys at the Diner. When
they ask what happened, he grins while
replying, "Hold on, fellas — don't ask
for details! There's a reputation at
stake here!" Mainly *his*, if they found
out that absolutely nothing happened.

HOW BIG A PHONY ARE YOU

TEST YOURSELF WITH THIS "PHONY QUIZ", AND SEE HOW YOU RATE. SCORE 10 POINTS FOR EACH CORRECT ANSWER

> **0-20** You are a real, down-to-earth, sincere, honest failure.
>
> **20-40** Promising, but your faith in phoniness needs strengthening.
>
> **40-60** You're a sweetie-beauty phony through and through, baby!

(1) When you are in a French Restaurant for the first time and you can't read the menu, you should **A.** Ask the waiter to translate, **B.** Order something and hope for the best, or **C.** Tell the waiter, "I'll leave it up to you, Pierre—you always know what I like!"

(2) If you are chosen as the Editor of the Class Yearbook, you should dedicate it to **A.** Some famous alumnus of your school, **B.** The outstanding member of your class, or **C.** The teacher who is about to flunk you in a tough subject.

(3) When you are at a wedding of people you actually hardly even know, you should say **A.** "Which one is Sandra and which one is Melvin?", **B.** "I really don't know either one of them!"—or **C** "That marriage was made in heaven—they're two great kids!"

(4) When you take a date to a Modern Art Museum, you should say, "These paintings are **A.** Idiotic!", **B.** Far beyond my understanding!" or **C.** Hmmm—Interesting, very interesting!"

(5) When you have no date on a Saturday night, you should **A.** Go to the movies with your best girlfriend, **B.** Go to the movies with your mother, or **C.** Go with either one . . . only talk loudly during the show about how your career leaves you absolutely no time for any kind of social life.

(6) While vacationing at a fancy Resort Hotel, you should **A.** Try to make friends, **B.** Enjoy all of the hotel facilities, or **C.** Have yourself paged every half hour.

We're not bothering to publish the correct answers since a true Phony would cheat anyhow!

Get Those Trouble-Makers Out Of Hollywood!

This Month's PHONY EDITORIAL

Just as that fearless journalist Émile Zola felt compelled to restore the reputation of Capt. Dreyfus, so your Editor feels compelled to protect the image of that land we phonies love so dearly . . . Hollywood. For years, we have looked for inspiration to the movie folk who have contributed so much toward making "Phony-ism" a way of life. Yet there are those among them who would destroy this gilt and lamé edifice of Phonydom. This attack on Hollywood is subtle, but make no mistake—this attack is in deadly earnest. J'accuse—MR. & MRS. FREDRIC MARCH!

* * * * *

Recently, a newspaper reported that the Marches have been happily married for 30 years! What's the meaning of this? Is this any way for a movie actor's name to appear in print—involved in a normal, happy marriage? This is an out-and-out betrayal of the Phony Hollywood Way Of Life—and to make it even worse, it comes from an Academy Award Winner!!

Let us further examine how Mr. March is defacing the hard-won Hollywood image: First, there is no record in any column, news story or fan mag that the Marches have ever considered a divorce! No one has ever seen them quarrel in public! Now what kind of Hollywood people are these? And what's more, Mr. March always displays humility and even sincerity when being interviewed! He has never once hit a photographer or reporter! He has never once had a fist fight in a night club! He has never once walked off a movie set in a fit of rage! And the home-life of the Marches is even worse—a positive insult to the Hollywood mentality! They've never had a single wild party! Some of their friends are actually not in show biz! They never plot against other stars or even start ugly rumors about them!

It all adds up to a scathing indictment of these two irresponsible people who are single-handedly destroying the image built by such Hollywood greats as Fatty Arbuckle and Errol Flynn. Let's keep Hollywood the Paradise of Phonies we love so well! Let's give our Stars, Starlets, Directors and Producers the freedom to be the phonies we've come to respect and admire. People like Mr. and Mrs. Fredric March are a menace!

We won't be happy until we've seen the first sly innuendo or unfounded item about them in some gossip column.

PHONY'S NEWS PHOTOS

Candid Studies Of "Phoniness" From The Newsfronts Around The World

NEW MISS AMERICA CROWNED

Laura Lee Lutz, the new "Miss America", shown here being congratulated by Sarah Sue Svelt, the girl she defeated for the title. "I really don't deserve this. There were much prettier girls," said Miss America. "She deserved it. I'm glad she won. She's a great kid," said the runner-up.

DEAN OF MEDICAL SCHOOL LECTURES A M A CONVENTION

Dr. Michael Smith, Dean of Yarvard Medical School, as he delivered his lecture, "America's Crying Need For More Doctors." Dr. Smith had to cut his speech short in order to return to Yarvard for a meeting to set their religious quotas for the coming term.

SENATOR GOLDWATER EXPLAINS VIEWS ON POVERTY

Senator Barry Goldwater as he explained his views on poverty at a Press Interview recently. "It's the individual's fault if he's poor," stated the Senator. "All you need to be successful is ambition and initiative!" The remarks were made before the multi-million dollar Department Store started by his grandfather years ago, and inherited by Sen. Goldwater.

CHIANG KAI-SHEK DELIVERS
ANNUAL MESSAGE TO TROOPS

Chiang Kai-shek delivering his annual morale message to his troops. "We will return to the Chinese mainland, and we will destroy the Reds!" Chiang promised his troops for the 19th straight year.

THE INQUIRING PHONY PHOTOGRAPHER

This Month's Question:
"What Do You Like Most About Your Work?"

RICHARD CARVER
New York City, N.Y.

I love the salesmanship involved in my work, and the pleasure I get from giving people the old soft soap and playing on their weaknesses. But nothing compares to the big thrill I get when I finally persuade some confused person to take something they really don't need. Yes, that's what I love best about being a fashionable Park Avenue Surgeon.

LEFTY GORKIN
Detroit, Michigan

It's the feeling of being a kid again. When you belt one out of the park or make a difficult running one-handed catch—that's living! Yes, I really love baseball, and I just can't wait until my team comes across with that one hundred thousand dollar contract that I am holding out for, so I can report to the training camp in Miami Beach.

KIM ZOFTIC
Hollywood, California

I adore my position as a "Starlet." Every night, I go to some fabulous party, meet terribly exciting people and have a ball. They say I have a wonderful future ahead of me. I just hope the studio doesn't get any idiotic ideas—like putting me into a movie. Golly, that would just about ruin my whole career.

85

Dear Sweetie

ADVICE TO THE PHONIES

by Sweetie Claghorn,
Phony Editor,
—and a Beautiful
Human Being

Dear Sweetie:

I'm tired of having the "right kind of job" and wearing the "right kind of Ivy League clothes" and being seen in the "right kind of places"! In other words, I'm sick of being a "Phony Conformist"! What can I do?
E.G.

Dear E.G.:

I suggest you quit your job and buy yourself some dungarees and start being seen in Greenwich Village Coffee Houses. In other words, you can become a "Phony NON-Conformist"!

Dear Sweetie:

Whenever I see an Ingmar Bergman movie, I never know what's going on. Afterwards, all my friends analyze and discuss it, but when they ask for my opinion, I just stand there looking like an idiot. Help me!
M.O.

Dear M.O.:

Next time they ask, look misty-eyed, sigh and say, "It was such a deep, meaningful, personal experience that I'd rather not discuss it!"

Dear Sweetie:

I have a problem. I am the mother of an 18 year old girl, and I've given her all the better things in life—a mink stole, a red M.G., charge accounts and vacations in Miami Beach. But no matter how hard I try, she persists in wasting hour after hour studying, she is an honor student, and she wants to become a teacher. Where have I failed her as a Mother?
Mrs. A.B.

Dear Mrs. A.B.:

Don't blame yourself. You did the best you could, and that's all that counts. If she wants to ruin her life, let her.

Dear Sweetie:

When is it proper to shake with the right hand, and when is it proper to shake—Hollywood Style—with the left hand?
R.Z.

Dear R.Z.:

Although the left hand shake is the traditional phony greeting, you are mistaken in calling it the "Hollywood Style." The Hollywood Style Greeting—for friends and total strangers alike—is a hug and a kiss.

Dear Sweetie:

Last week, I took a date to a fancy restaurant. When the check came, I pulled out a huge roll of bills, peeled off a fifty and paid it. She's refused to go out with me since. Do you think I was too obvious in trying to impress her?
N.M.

Dear N.M.:

The trouble is—you didn't impress her at all. Anyone who pays cash in a restaurant must be on the verge of bankruptcy. When you take out your next date, use a credit card.

Dear Sweetie:

Your column irritates me. Why should people want to be phonies? They should be real and honest—like me. I don't want to be something I'm not. Nor do I desire things I cannot have. I have found true happiness in my wife and 8 kids, and great satisfaction in my job as a simple Janitor.
W.L.

Dear W.L.:

I admire you very much. Your argument shows that you are one of the biggest phonies who ever wrote to us. Congrats!

Dear Sweetie:

I am engaged to a boy who is a phony through-and-through. I can't believe a word he tells me, and his promises are worthless. What should I do?
P.L.

Dear P.L.:

Marry the boy immediately! He has the makings of a great Business Executive!

86

A FINE DAY IN THE CITY

Here we go with the first of a three-part series on "Parties" — in which we'll also look at "Kids' Parties" and "Teenage Parties." But first, we cover . . . .

THE LIGHTER SIDE OF

Gee, I can't wait to grow up so I can go to "Big People" parties . . .

ADULT PARTIES

ARTIST & WRITER: DAVE BERG

... and act like a kid!!

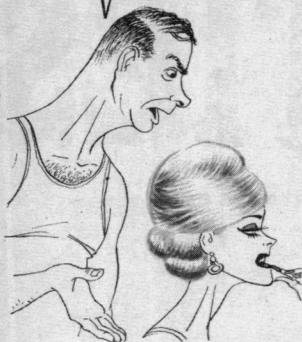

Happy Anniversary, dear!

Same to you, darling! And I ask you, isn't this quiet dinner by ourselves much better than having a party?

I'll say it is! Last year we almost got a **divorce** because of a party we threw. Frankly, I can't **stand** the way you behave at shindigs!

Look who's talking! You embarrass me to **death** the way you carry on every time!

Yeah—well, I felt that one more party with you and we'd both be drinking a new concoction . . . **"Marriage on the Rocks . . ."**

98

Good night everybody! Thank you for coming!

You lecherous dirty old man! I saw you pinch Marcia!

I did no such thing, you suspicious old bag! I never **touched** Marcia! I was flirting with **Rosie** all night!

I could have fallen through the **floor** when you told everybody I was thirty-two!

So what did you want me to do—tell 'em the **truth** . . . that you're really thirty-eight!?

Thank goodness this party is over. I couldn't go through with **another** one like it for a whole **year**!

But look at all the good **food** and **drinks** that are left over. What are we going to do with all **that**?

Well, tomorrow night we could invite in the Millers and the Reillys and the Finns. They'll help us get rid of the stuff!

And while we're at it, we owe invitations to the Wagners and the Smiths and the Dunns and the Formans. So we might as well make a party of it!

Well . . . that was the shortest year on record!!

IN A DEPARTMENT STORE

TUNES OF GORY DEPT.

As long as we can remember, Safety Songs have always played an important part in the education of children. Grammar school teachers are constantly leading their classes in the singing of tunes which tell kids how to live safely amidst the many and varied pitfalls of life. However, a thought recently occurred to us : mainly

CHILDren'S
ARE USUALLY BASED

...like playing with matches:

BAD, BAD MATCHES
(to the tune of "Frère Jacques")

Bad, bad matches,
   Bad, bad matches,
I touched you,
   I touched you.
You made quite a fire,
   There goes brother Meyer . . .
Toodle-ooo,
Toodle-oo.

safety songs
ON OLD-FASHIONED SUBJECTS

ARTIST: JOE ORLANDO   **WRITER: LARRY SIEGEL**

...and touching nasty plants:

MY BODY HAS CALAMINE LOTION
(to the tune of *"My Bonnie Lies Over The Ocean"*)

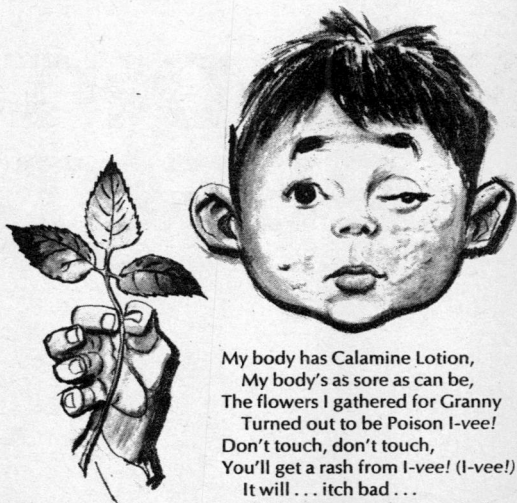

My body has Calamine Lotion,
   My body's as sore as can be,
The flowers I gathered for Granny
   Turned out to be Poison I-*vee!*
Don't touch, don't touch,
   You'll get a rash from I-*vee!* (I-*vee!*)
It will . . . itch bad . . .
And it looks worse than ac-*nee!*

YOU FUNNY IODINE
(to the tune of "My Darling Clementine")

In the chest there, in the bathroom,
O'er the sink whose faucets shine,
Stands a funny little bottle,
And we call it iodine.

Now we realize, of course, that playing with matches and drinking iodine and touching poison ivy and crossing in the middle of the block always have been and always will be dangerous. But we feel that,

UP-TO-DATE
SAFETY

Oh you funny, oh you funny,
   Oh, you funny iodine.
You don't taste good with a cookie
   But for booboos you're just fine.

times change, we should add **new** Safety Songs to Grammar school repertoires. Songs which are in
keeping with more **modern** safety problems in the Soaring Sixties. And so here are some suggested . . .

SONGS FOR CHILDREN

IT'S A GRAND OLD BAG
(to the tune of "You're A Grand Old Flag")

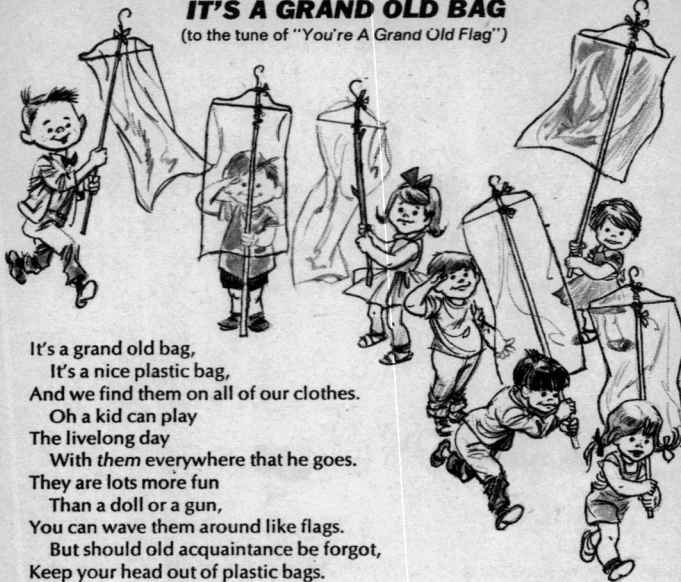

It's a grand old bag,
   It's a nice plastic bag,
And we find them on all of our clothes.
   Oh a kid can play
The livelong day
   With *them* everywhere that he goes.
They are lots more fun
   Than a doll or a gun,
You can wave them around like flags.
   But should old acquaintance be forgot,
Keep your head out of plastic bags.

ROAD-RAVAGED VALLEY
(to the tune of "Red River Valley")

In this valley I see they are working,
   They are building a Throughway, they say.
It will cut 'cross your yard and will just miss
   Your split ranch, which is twelve feet away.

     Do not play by the craters they're digging,
       For the craters are big and they're deep.
     If you fall into one you'll be buried,
       And you don't really need all that sleep.

        Do not touch all those funny explosives,
          Do not play with that dynamite cap.
        Otherwise you will find, like the Throughway,
          You'll be spread out all over the map.

I'VE GOT TO STOP SMOKING

(to the tune of "On Top Of Old Smoky")

I've got to stop smoking,
   My doctor has said,
Or else when I'm seven,
   I'm sure to be dead.

Cigarettes can cause cancer,
   And that makes no sense.
So I must stop stealing
   My dear Daddy's Kents.

Now here in the 60's,
   When going with chicks,
Cigarettes can bring status
   To a boy who is six.

But I must live clean now;
   At six life is ripe.
Cigarettes I will give up—
   And switch to a pipe!

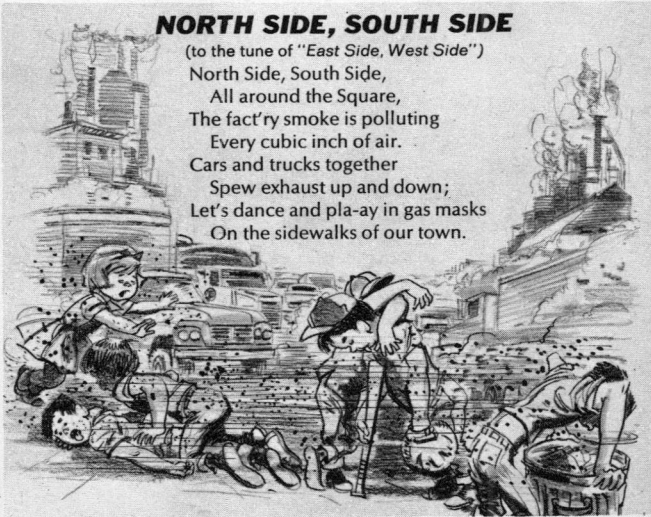

NORTH SIDE, SOUTH SIDE

(to the tune of "*East Side, West Side*")

North Side, South Side,
  All around the Square,
The fact'ry smoke is polluting
  Every cubic inch of air.
Cars and trucks together
  Spew exhaust up and down;
Let's dance and pla-ay in gas masks
  On the sidewalks of our town.

WHEN THE BOMB
COMES FALLING DOWN

(to the tune of "London Bridge Is Falling Down")

When the Bomb comes falling down,
Falling down, falling down,
When the Bomb comes falling down,
There'll be fallout.

Cover up your face and head,
Face and head, face and head,
Then put on your suit of lead,
'Cause there's fallout.

Do not stop to talk or play,
Talk or play, talk or play,
Find your shelter right away,
'Cause there's fallout.

Just admit your nearest kin,
Nearest kin, nearest kin,
Shoot down neighbors who want in,
'Cause there's fallout.

Wait until they sound All Clear,
Sound All Clear, sound All Clear,
Don't drink milk till late next year,
'Cause there's fallout.

BUCKLE UP YOUR
HELMET STRAP

(to the tune of *"Button Up Your Overcoat"*)

Buckle up your helmet strap,
Hide behind a tree;
There's a riot again
Down at P.S. 3.

Don't go near the picket line,
That's no place to be;
They may fracture your skull
Down at P.S. 3.

Beware of roughneck nuts *(mmm-mmm)*
Switchblade cuts *(mmm-mmm)*
Trooper's mutts *(mmm-mmm)*
You'll get a bite in your tummy-tum-tum-tum . . .

Keep away from flying rocks,
They may break your knee;
Life at school nowadays
Is like World War III.

119

A
MAD LOOK

AT WINTER SPORTS

ARTIST & WRITER: SERGIO ARAGONES

Most grownups have trouble understanding today's strange-sounding newspaper headli
so you can imagine how they probably affect kids . . . especially those whose knowle
of politics, geography and spelling may be lacking. Here, then, is our version of w
might be running through their simple, innocent little minds . . . as MAD presents

A CHILD'S
VIEW
OF NEWSPAPER
HEADLINES

ARTIST & WRITER:
AL JAFFEE

EXTRA ☆ The Daily News-Bungler ☆ **EXTRA**

VOL. CXIII No. 25,897   ALFREDSVILLE, WEDNESDAY, JULY 8, 1964   PRICE: 10 CENTS

GUERRILLAS ATTACK ON PLAIN OF JARS

LAOS, JULY 7 (AP) Guerrilla forces today attacked General Nu T. Chvay's government troops on The Plain of Jars, predicting heavy casualties...

BUILDING BOOM IN SUBURBS

Easy mortgage money continues to give ... to the housing industry as subur...

131

Embezzler Escapes To Brazil With 700 G's

NEW YORK, JULY 28 (*INS*) Irwin Sol Gilbert, former Treasurer of Shlock Industries, disappeared with $700,000 of company funds, it was learned today. It is rumored Gilbert was seen boarding a plane for Brazil, accompanied by...

SENATOR PROBES MISSILE GAP

CAPE KENNEDY, AUGUST 4 (*UPI*) Senator ...son P. Muckraker made a surprise ...n of this missile site to...n his ...d Govern...nds

SCHOOL TAX TO BE HIGHER

Voters of the Noxious School Di...

PARTY LEADERS SPLIT ON PLATFORM

SAN FRANCISCO, JULY 15 (*BO*) Republican Party leaders are still arguing among themselves plan for 1962 plat...

CAR POOLS EASE L.A. BUS STRIKE TENSION

LOS ANGELES, JUNE 2 (*RIP*) The threat to thousands of stranded commuters eased considerably today large numbers of organized

SOUTH VIETNAM ARMY HEADS REMOVED

SAIGON, AUG. 11 (*LP*) Three leaders of the South Vietnamese army were relieved of their duties today in a

SECTION TWO · NEUMANVILLE, TUESDAY, SEPTEMBER 22, 1964 · PAGE 17.

BRAVES SWEEP GIANT DOUBLE-HEADER

BOSTON, SEPT. 21 *(LP)* The Boston Braves took two from the San Francisco Giants today, before a crowd estimated as mostly drunk and disorderly with a ninth inning second-game riot developing wh

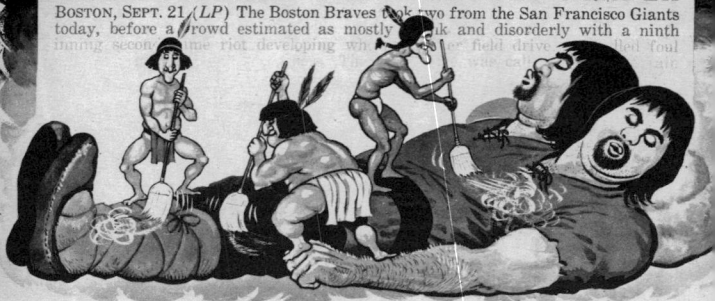

TEXAS GULF SULPHUR ANNOUNCES HUGE CANADIAN ORE DISCOVERY

PUSHUPSTOOT, ONTARIO, MAY 30 *(DJA)* Spokesmen for Texas Gulf Sulphur Co announced today that a discovery of mineral deposits on land

Since MAD's Official Article-Introduction Writer is ill this month, we've assigned Sidney Gwirtzman, MAD's Accountant, to serve as Guest Introduction Writer for the following article. Here is Mr. Gwirtzman's Introduction: *"The law provides a credit against tax dividends received from qualifying domestic corporations. This credit is equal to 4 percent of these dividends in excess of those which you may exclude from your income. The credit may not exceed: (a) the total income tax reduced by foreign tax credit; or (b) 4 percent of the . . ."* But enough of this hilarity. Let's save the jokes for the story as

MAD LOOKS AT A TYPICAL KIDDIE TV SHOW

ARTIST: MORT DRUCKER   WRITER: LARRY SIEGEL

I hear Uncle Nutzy is going to a **Masquerade Party** after the show!

Really? Is he going to wear what he's wearing now?

No, he's going in a **funny costume!** Those are his **street clothes!**

Okay, gang! Let's start off the show with our daily prayer! Repeat after me . . . Bless Mommy and Daddy and Brother and Sister and our house and our milk and **especially** our delicious, lip-smacking **Yummy-Cream Cookies**—put out by the Monopoly Biscuit Company— a fine American Corporation, and a great sponsor . . .

Now, our guests in the studio are going to show our friends at home **how** we're going to get Daddy to **give** us the money—

That's right, Lisa! We're going to have **convulsions**!

Very good, Sally! We're going to hold our **breath** till our face turns blue!

And if all that fails, you know what we're going to do? We're going to **pick Daddy's pockets**! Right, kids? Won't that be fun?

Oh, say, kids! There have been some complaints from various "square" parent groups about us selling you "Teeny"—the little **baby** doll that belongs to Bubbie and her boy-friend doll, Ben. You know . . . they think it's a rather **unhealthy arrangement**! So guess what the Bubbie Doll Company is going to do in order to make everything **wonderful** and **decent** again? For just $31.00, you can get Daddy to buy you a "**Preacher Doll**" and you can stage your very own **wedding** for Bubbie and Ben! Better late than never, we always say! Ha-ha!

NOW ONLY $31.00
THE NEW IMPROVED ®PREACHER DOLL!

BE THE FIRST ON YOUR BLOCK!

ALSO FOR A LIMITED TIME ONLY! WITNESS DOLLS ONLY $27.59 EACH!

IT'S HERE, Boys and girls!! The great new fun-toy you've been waiting for! "DEATH—26"!! Yes, kids, "Death—26" is 26 real fun-weapons combined into one magnificent toy! It's a combination rifle, machine gun, rocket-launcher, grenade-thrower, bazooka, mortar, H-bomb detonator, and so much **more!**

Can't you just picture yourself destroying the entire **Russian Army** with your "Death—26"?

. . . and laying to waste ¾ of the world . . . ?

. . . and eliminating all the **competitors** of Yummy Cream Cookies . . . ?

. . . and all the other **Kiddie Show Emcees** except your Uncle Nutzy? **You bet you can!!**

"Death—26" is a product of Educational Toys Corporation and costs just $212.00 wherever all fine toys are sold! And, kids, remember our sensational **"Free Trial Offer"**! We'll send you a **"Death—26"** at no **charge** for **one whole week!** Think of what you can **do** with it: Frighten your friends, scare shell-shocked war veterans . . . and even make Daddy **come across** with $212.00 so you can **keep** your **"Death—26"** toy after the free trial week is over . . . **OR ELSE!!**

Here we go with the third and last installment of "Parties"— which included "Adult Parties" and "Teenage Parties"! Mainly, here is...

THE LIGHTER SIDE OF

kids' parties

ARTIST & WRITER: DAVE BERG

154

Hold it, kids! Go outside and **come in again**! I want to get a shot of everybody **arriving** for the party . . .

Step **aside**, kids! I want to dolly in for a close-up of Mitch **opening his presents**! And Mitchel . . . close that box, and **open it again** while I'm shooting . . . then smile!

Nancy, put your blindfold back on for a shot of "**Pin The Tail On The Donkey**" . . . only **this** time, pin the tail on the **Birthday Boy**!

Hold it, kids, while I get a **long-shot** of this! Mitch, get in the middle, and act like you're **embarrassed**!

The party is in the playroom **downstairs, children!** As for you **mothers,** I have some **cocktails** in the **living room** while you're waiting! **Help yourselves!**

Well . . . how'd you like the **Kiddie Party?**

It wash shwell! HIC

163

A
MAD
LOOK AT
SIGNS OF THE TIMES

ARTIST: BOB CLARKE

Today's road signs are very often confusing, illegible, or just plain hard to understand. On the theory that a picture is worth a thousand words (Especially for clods who can't read!), we offer the following MAD suggestion for improving road safety: Mainly, make use of more—

PICTURE ROAD SIGNS

WRITER: AL JAFFEE

HARD to understand WORD SIGNS

BUS STOP

NO HEAVY TRUCKS

Does this sign indicate that the bus stops over it—in mid-air? Or does it mean that the bus is going up after it stops?

Does this mean that light trucks are okay? And how light? How about a heavy truck transporting lights? That's sure a light truck!

PAY TOLL

EASY to understand PICTURE SIGNS

This sign is instantly understood by anyone who drives by. It indicates School Children in the area—so drive carefully.

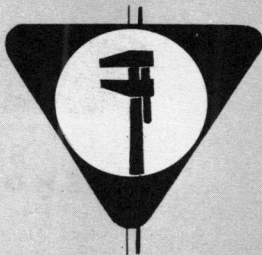

This sign is immediately understood by Frenchmen, Englishmen, Germans, etc. Used in Europe, it means a Service Station ahead.

M E N WORKING

SOFT
SHOULDER

FLOOD
AREA

NO RIGHT TURN

REST ROOMS AHEAD

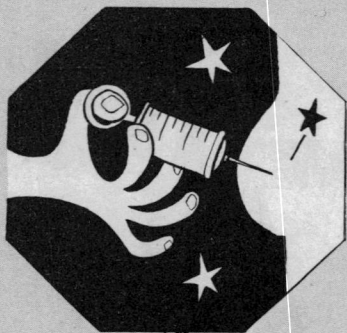

DEAD END

LOW FLYING PLANES

**DEER
CROSSING**

**BUMPY
ROAD**

LOW
BRIDGE

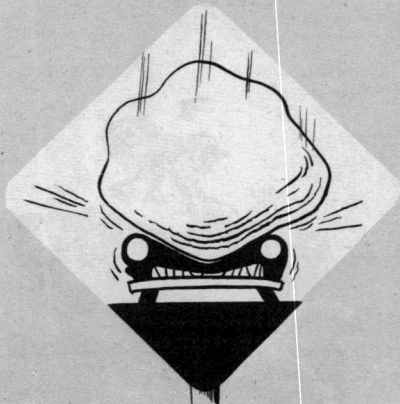

FALLEN ROCK
ZONE

THERE IS STILL ANOTHER AREA WHERE "PICTURE SIGNS" CAN BE HELPFUL: WITH CITIES AND TOWNS GROWING TO THE POINT OF TOUCHING EACH OTHER, IT IS BECOMING MORE DIFFICULT TO TELL WHEN YOU LEAVE ONE AND ENTER ANOTHER. A "PICTURE SIGN" WOULD INSTANTLY SHOW YOU WHERE YOU ARE.

MIAMI BEACH

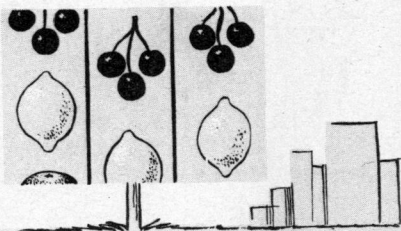

LAS VEGAS

WASHINGTON, D.C.

HOUSTON

RENO

LOS ANGELES

days gone by, merchants and craftsmen used to hang out signs depicting symbolic objects
at quickly identified the nature of their business. The cobbler hung out a shoe, the ocu-
st—a pair of glasses, the watchmaker—a clock, etc. Nearly all of these types of signs
e gone now, but we'd like to bring them back and up-date them to cover some of the rackets
at have sprung up since those good old days. Here, then, are a few MAD suggestions for ...

Up-To-Date Symbolic
BUSINESS SIGNS

Mannie Schlepper
ACTORS' AGENT

WRITER: DON REILLY

ADVERTISING
EXECUTIVES
CLUB

Society
of
Drama Critics

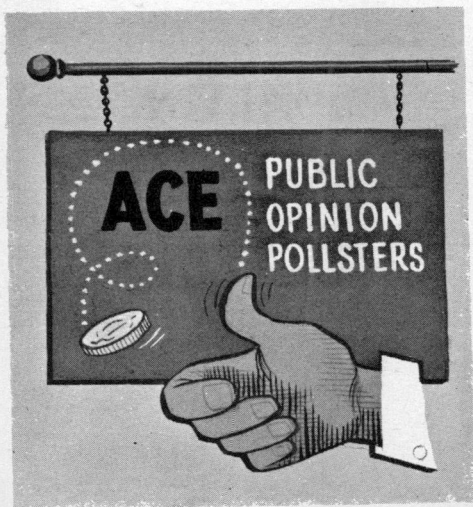

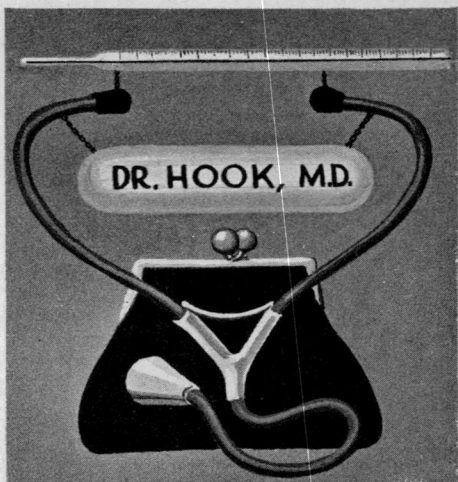

QUALITY USED CARS

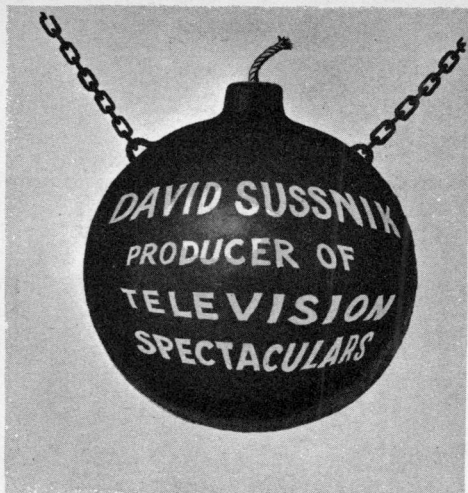

DAVID SUSSNIK
PRODUCER OF
TELEVISION
SPECTACULARS

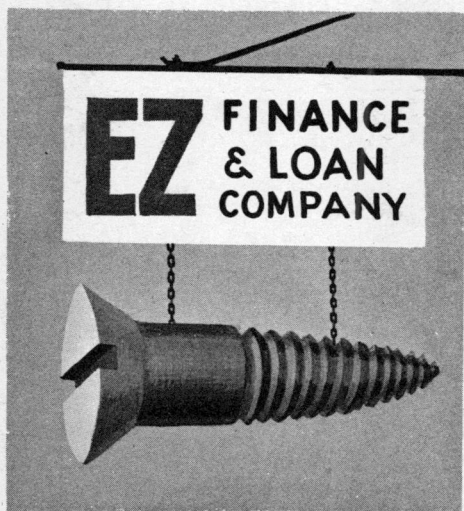

EZ FINANCE
& LOAN
COMPANY

PART III

You think you gotta be on your guard because Madison Avenue is sneaky when it comes to commercials and ads? Well, next time you're out shopping, take a closer look at those signs in store windows. If necessary, have someone read them to you. Or better yet, just let whoever is reading this article to you continue, and you'll see that your local merchant is pulling some sneaky tricks on his own. Mainly, he's faking you out with these

WRITER: DICK DE BARTOLO

SNEAKY SIGNS

GOING OUT OF BUSINESS!
IN 1967 OR 1968 IF THINGS DON'T PICK UP A BIT

SALE! SALE! SALE!
OUR DOORS CLOSE TONIGHT!
—AND OPEN TOMORROW AS USUAL AT 8:00 A.M.

BUSINESS IS SO LOUSY, WE ONLY WISH WE WERE
FORCED TO VACATE!

WE LOST OUR LEASE
IT WAS RIGHT IN OUR
TOP DRAWER JUST YESTERDAY!

50% to 60% OFF
ON PRICES WE
RECENTLY BOOSTED
50% TO 60%

WE WOULDN'T MAKE ANY MONEY AT ALL IF WE WERE REALLY
SELLING BELOW ACTUAL WHOLESALE!

DRASTIC REDUCTIONS
IN QUALITY

DON'T COME IN HERE IF YOU'RE EXPECTING
DISCOUNTS!!!

Over the years, Man has relied on signs for important information. However, today, America has become a "Sign-Happy" nation. F'rinstance, would we be any less-informed if we were to do away with these...

USELESS SIGNS

WRITER: DICK DE BARTOLO

BRIDGE
OUT

PARKING

FULL

185

IN A LAS VEGAS HOTEL LOBBY

ARTIST: GEORGE WOODBRIDGE